Just-in-Time
for Operators

SHOPFLOOR SERIES

Just-in-Time
for Operators

CREATED BY

The Productivity Press
Development Team

Productivity Press
PORTLAND, OREGON

Additional copies of this book and a learning package for leading a book study group are available from the publisher. Discounts are available for multiple copies through the Sales Department (800-394-6868). Address all other inquiries to:

Productivity Press
P.O. Box 13390
Portland OR 97213-0390
United States of America
Telephone: 503-235-0600
Fax: 503-235-0909
E-mail: service@ppress.com

Cover by Carla Refojo
Cover illustration by Gary Ragaglia
Page design and composition by Stanton Design
Printed and bound by BookCrafters in the United States of America

Library of Congress Cataloging-in-Publication Data

Just-in-time for operators / created by the Productivity Press Development Team.
     p. cm. — (Shopfloor series)
    Includes bibliographical references.
    ISBN 1-56327-133-8 (pbk.)
    1. Just-in-time systems. I. Productivity Press Development Team. II. Series.
TS157.4.J86 1998
658.5′6—dc21   97–52252
                                                       CIP

03 02 01 00 99 98 10 9 8 7 6 5 4 3 2 1

Contents

Chapter 2. Basic Concepts of Just-in-Time

Chapter 3. Process Improvement and Standardization

Chapter 4. Support Techniques for Just-in-Time

Chapter 5. Reflections and Conclusions

Publisher's Message

Just-in-time manufacturing is an approach that can dramatically boost your company's competitiveness by eliminating waste from the production process. The change from traditional large-lot production to just-in-time requires a new understanding about what adds value for the customer and what does not. And although management determines the manufacturing approach, frontline operators and assembly people play a key role in making it happen. This book is intended to share basic knowledge that will help you participate effectively in this change.

As you read this book, you will realize that just-in-time is not really one approach, but a set of approaches that supports a different way of operating a factory. These approaches are so intertwined that it can be difficult to know where to start. Chapter 1 lays a foundation with some basic definitions related to just-in-time — and the reasons it is so important for U.S. companies and their employees. Then, in Chapter 2, we first address leveled production, because it creates a direct link between production processes and the estimated needs of customers. The build-what-the-customer-orders philosophy of leveled production is transmitted throughout the plant by an inventory control system such as kanban.

Chapter 3 describes another key aspect of just-in-time: improvement of the process to eliminate waste. A key aspect of process improvement for just-in-time is arrangement of equipment in a process flow sequence. This simple change has a big effect on how people interact with equipment, and often entails learning new skills to operate several different machines in a process sequence. The new way of performing the process is standardized by the people in the workplace. The new standard makes the work in each process predictable and serves as the base for further improvements.

Chapter 4 briefly describes the 5S system, visual management, quick changeover, mistake-proofing, total productive maintenance, and other techniques that make just-in-time operation possible. Chapter 5 helps the reader review his or her learning and suggests additional resources for exploring key topics.

It is important to remember as you read that this material is a general orientation to a complex topic. Implementation and mastery of the just-in-time approach requires a deeper understanding of the production mechanism. The implementation process is best supported by experienced consultants and trainers who can tailor it to your company's specific situation and help address the issues that may be raised by this change.

This book incorporates a number of features that will help you make the most of it. Each chapter begins with an overview of the contents. The book uses many illustrations to share information and examples in a visual way. Icons in the margin help identify key points to remember in each section. And questions built into the text provide a framework for applying what you've learned to your own situation.

One of the most effective ways to use this book is to read and discuss it with other employees in group learning sessions. We have deliberately planned the book so that it can be used this way, with chunks of information that can be covered in a series of short sessions. Each chapter includes reflection questions to stimulate group discussion. A Learning Package is also available, which includes a leader's guide, overhead transparencies to summarize major points, and color slides showing examples of just-in-time techniques in different companies.

The just-in-time approach is simple and universal. It works in companies all over the world. Today, the basic principles of just-in-time have been used to eliminate waste in all types of manufacturing, assembly, and even service industries. We hope this book and Learning Package will tell you what you need to know to make your participation in a just-in-time implementation active and personally rewarding.

Acknowledgments

This book is modeled after the instructional design developed by Melanie Rubin, formerly of Productivity, Inc. The form and content of the Shopfloor Series books have been heavily influenced by input from Productivity customers, including participants in two focus groups, readers who reviewed the manuscript, and respondents to our telephone survey. Dee Tadlock of Read Right Systems also gave extensive instructional design input and review to this format.

The development of *Just-in-Time for Operators* has been a strong team effort. Within Productivity Press, Steven Ott and Diane Asay played major roles in product definition and support. Karen Jones served as project manager and developer, advised by Productivity Consulting Group members Raymond Louis, Frank Hammitt, Rich Niedermeier, and Connie Dyer. Bill Stanton created the book and cover design for the series; cover composition was by Carla Refojo and cover illustration by Gary Ragaglia of The Vision Group. Susan Swanson managed the prepress production and manufacturing, with editorial assistance from Sheryl Rose. Page composition was done by Stanton Design. Graphic illustrations were created by Lee Smith, and cartoon illustrations were created by Hannah Bonner.

Finally, the staff at Productivity Press wishes to acknowledge the good work of the many people who are now in the process of implementing the just-in-time system in their own organizations. We welcome any feedback about this book, as well as input about how we can continue to serve you in your JIT implementation efforts.

Steven Ott
President

Karen Jones
Senior Development Editor

Getting Started

The Purpose of This Book

Key Point

Just-in-Time for Operators *was written to give you the information you need to participate in implementing the just-in-time manufacturing approach in your workplace.* You are a valued member of your company's team; your knowledge, support, and participation are essential to the success of any major effort in your organization.

The paragraph you have just read explains the author's purpose in writing this book. It also explains why your company may wish you to read this book. But why are *you* reading this book? This question is even more important. What you get out of this book largely depends on your purpose in reading it.

You may be reading this book because your team leader or manager asked you to do so. Or you may be reading it because you think it will provide information that will help you in your work. By the time you finish Chapter 1, you will have a better idea of how the information in this book can help you and your company eliminate waste and serve your customers more effectively.

What This Book Is Based On

BACKGROUND
INFO

This book is about the just-in-time manufacturing approach, which was first developed at Toyota Motor Company. Since 1979, Productivity has brought information about the just-in-time approach to the United States through study tours, conferences, newsletters, training, and consulting. Productivity Press supports just-in-time education with books and other materials on this important subject. (See pages 66–69 for a list of related resources.)

Just-in-Time for Operators draws on a wide variety of Productivity's resources. Its aim is to present the main concepts and techniques of just-in-time in a simple, illustrated format that is easy to read and understand.

Figure I-1. Two Ways to Use This Book

Two Ways to Use This Book

BACKGROUND INFO

There are at least two ways to use this book:

1. As the reading material for a learning group or study group process within your company.

2. For learning on your own.

Productivity Press offers a Learning Package that uses *Just-in-Time for Operators* as the foundation reading material for a learning group. Your company may decide instead to design its own learning group process based on *Just-in-Time for Operators*. Or, you may read this book for individual learning without formal group discussion.

How to Get the Most Out of Your Reading

Becoming Familiar with This Book as a Whole

There are a few steps you can follow to make it easier to absorb the information in this book. Take as much time as you need to become familiar with the material. First, get a "big picture" view of the book by doing the following:

How-to Steps

1. Scan the Table of Contents to see how *Just-in-Time for Operators* is arranged.

2. Read the rest of this section for an overview of the book's contents.

3. Flip through the book to get a feel for its style, flow, and design. Notice how the chapters are structured and glance at the pictures.

Becoming Familiar with Each Chapter

After you have a sense of the structure of *Just-in-Time for Operators*, prepare yourself to study one chapter at a time. For each chapter, we suggest you follow these steps to get the most out of your reading:

How-to Steps

1. Read the "Chapter Overview" on the first page to see where the chapter is going.

2. Flip through the chapter, looking at the way it is laid out. Notice the bold headings and the key points flagged in the margins.

3. Now read the chapter. How long this takes depends on what you already know about the content, and what you are trying to get out of your reading. Enhance your reading by doing the following:

   • Use the margin assists to help you follow the flow of information.

   • If the book is your own, use a highlighter to mark key information and answers to your questions about the material. If the book is not your own, take notes on a separate piece of paper.

   • Answer the "Take Five" questions in the text. These will help you absorb the information by reflecting on how you might implement it.

4. Read the "Chapter Summary" to confirm what you have learned. If you don't remember something in the summary, find that section in the chapter and review it.

5. Finally, read the "Reflections" questions at the end of the chapter. Think about these questions and write down your answers.

Figure I-2. Giving Your Brain a Framework for Learning

How a Reading Strategy Works

When reading a book, many people think they should start with the first word and read straight through until the end. This is not usually the best way to learn from a book. The steps described on pages xiv and xv are a strategy for making your reading easier, more fun, and more effective.

Key Point

Reading strategy is based on two simple points about the way people learn. The first point is this: *It's difficult for your brain to absorb new information if it does not have a structure to place it in.* As an analogy, imagine trying to build a house without first putting up a framework.

Like building a frame for a house, you can give your brain a framework for the new information in the book by getting an overview of the contents and then flipping through the materials. Within each chapter, you repeat this process on a smaller scale by reading the overview, key points, and headings before reading the text.

Key Point

The second point about learning is this: *It is a lot easier to learn if you take in the information one layer at a time, instead of trying to absorb it all at once.* It's like finishing the walls of a house: First you lay down a coat of primer. When it's dry, you apply a coat of paint, and later a final finish coat.

Using the Margin Assists

As you've noticed by now, this book uses small images called margin assists to help you follow the information in each chapter. There are five types of margin assists:

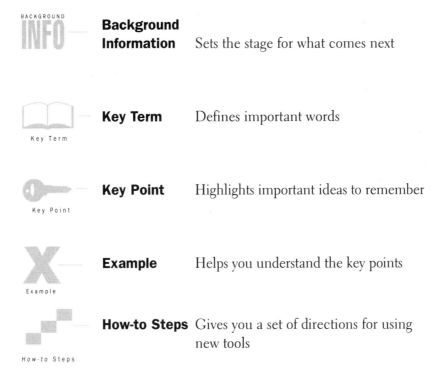

Background Information Sets the stage for what comes next

Key Term Defines important words

Key Point Highlights important ideas to remember

Example Helps you understand the key points

How-to Steps Gives you a set of directions for using new tools

Overview of the Contents

Getting Started (pages xiii–xviii)

This is the section you're reading now. It explains the purpose of *Just-in-Time for Operators* and how it was written. Then it shares tips for getting the most out of your reading. Finally, it presents this overview of each chapter.

Chapter 1. An Introduction to Just-in-Time (pages 1–14)

Chapter 1 introduces and defines just-in-time manufacturing and the kinds of waste it helps eliminate. It also explains how the just-in-time approach benefits companies and their employees, and defines processes and operations as a framework for the rest of the book.

Chapter 2. Basic Concepts of Just-in-Time (pages 15–28)

Chapter 2 explains key mechanical concepts of just-in-time manufacturing, including leveled production, takt time, and kanban systems.

Chapter 3. Process Improvement and Standardization (pages 29–46)

Chapter 3 describes process improvements to eliminate waste. Topics include process-based equipment layout, multi-machine operation, and autonomation. It describes how standardization helps make processes predictable and supports continuous improvement.

Chapter 4. Support Techniques for Just-in-Time (pages 47–62)

Chapter 4 covers essential methods that make JIT possible, beginning with the 5S system and visual management. Quick changeover, poka-yoke (mistake-proofing), total productive maintenance, and new performance measures are also described.

Chapter 5. Reflections and Conclusions pages 63–69)

Chapter 5 presents reflections on and conclusions to this book. It also describes opportunities for further learning about just-in-time and related techniques.

Chapter 1

An Introduction to Just-in-Time

Figure 1-1. Delivering What Customers Want, When They Want, in the Quantity They Want

What Is Just-in-Time?

Key Term

Just-in-time (often called JIT for short) is a manufacturing approach that enables a company to produce the products its customers want, when they want them, and in the amount they want (see Figure 1-1).

Key Point

Just-in-time differs from the mass production approach used by many companies. Mass production is designed to produce large lots of identical products, which are stored and later shipped to customers as they are ordered. In contrast, *the JIT approach allows a company to produce a variety of products in smaller quantities, with a shorter lead time, to meet specific customer needs.*

Implementing JIT often means dramatic changes in the way production processes are carried out. This transition is likely to involve a new way of controlling the production schedule based on customer needs. It will probably mean a new equipment layout and new roles for operators. This chapter explains why these and other changes are worthwhile for you and your company. It will also introduce you to basic JIT concepts and principles, and prepare you for learning about JIT techniques in later chapters.

Type	Examples
Defects	Scrap, rework, replacement production, inspection
Waiting	Stockouts, lot processing delays, equipment downtime, capacity bottlenecks
Processing	Unnecessary or incorrect processing
Overproduction	Manufacturing items for which there are no orders
Movement	Human motions that are unnecessary or straining
Inventory	Excess raw material, WIP, or finished goods
Transport	Carrying WIP long distances, inefficient transport
Unused employee creativity	Lost time, ideas, skills, improvements

Figure 1-2. Waste in Manufacturing

Why JIT Is Important

Key Point

Customers today want a variety of products in just the quantities they need. They also expect high quality, a good price, and speedy delivery of their orders. *JIT manufacturing helps companies become more competitive by producing the desired variety while keeping costs low, quality high, and lead time minimal.* It does this by eliminating waste in the manufacturing process.

Recognizing Waste

Key Term

Waste is any element of the manufacturing process that adds cost without adding value to the product. Waste not only costs money, it also extends the lead time for building the product and delivering it to the customer. And it keeps the company from doing more productive things with its resources. Figure 1-2 lists eight major wastes in manufacturing.

TAKE FIVE

Take five minutes to think about these questions and to write down your answers:

- What wastes can you see in your process? Which do you think are the most serious problems at your company?

Figure 1-3. Inventory Covers Up Other Problems

Overproduction Is Waste

Key Term

BACKGROUND INFO

Overproduction happens when companies create products or work-in-process (WIP) for which they do not currently have orders. It is one of the worst forms of waste, because it generates another waste—excess inventory.

Companies often overproduce when they make products in large lots. Large lots are used because changeovers take too long to make frequent setups economical. However, companies often forget about the costs associated with this excess inventory. And they don't always realize that processing unneeded items lengthens the lead time for the quantity the customer wants. Chapter 4 describes quick changeover techniques that allow companies to produce small quantities economically.

Inventory Is Waste

Key Term

Inventory is an accumulation of products, WIP, or materials at any stage of the process. Many companies plan for extra inventory (safety stock) to cover for problems such as

- Production imbalances
- Equipment downtime
- Late deliveries from suppliers
- Long setup times
- Defects (see Figure 1-3)

Key Point

But inventory is waste. It is especially bad because it hides other problems. When safety stock exists, people are not motivated to make improvements.

Key Point

Furthermore, *the existence of inventory at any stage of the process causes additional wastes such as:*

- **Transport:** When processes make items that aren't used immediately, the items must be moved and stored. Companies use conveyors, forklifts, or other devices to move inventory around between processes. This transport adds cost to the process without adding any value.

- **Storage:** Companies must pay for space to store inventory (including space for WIP sitting between processes) and people to manage it. Again, this use of valuable resources does not add value.

- **Damage:** Keeping inventory can lead to quality problems because inventory can be damaged in handling or storage, or can deteriorate over time. Some items may even become obsolete and useless.

- **Delay:** Working on in-process inventory in large lots results in delays, because no items can move on to the next operation until all the items in the lot are processed.

Key Point

Finally, *inventory is wasteful in itself because it ties up the company's resources:* people, equipment, materials, and energy are required to produce every item. And, as long as inventory remains in the plant or the warehouse, the company is not repaid for its investment in these resources.

Figure 1-4 on the next page summarizes the types of waste caused by overproduction and inventory.

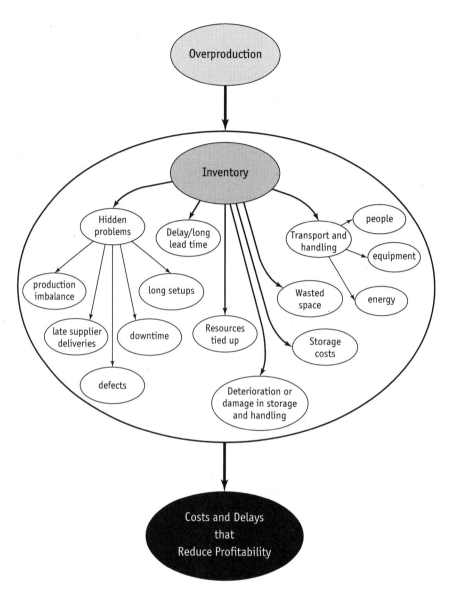

Figure 1-4. Waste from Overproduction and Inventory

Figure 1-5. The Trouble with Inventory

Key Point

Inventory waste affects every production process that depends on a previous process for materials or parts. When a plant has many processes, each handling items in large lots, the cumulative waste of time and money is enormous (see Figure 1-5).

To eliminate this waste, companies use just-in-time manufacturing methods to build and deliver just the inventory the customer needs, when needed, in the amount needed. This is achieved for the final process through an approach called leveled production, and managed between earlier processes through an inventory control system such as kanban. Both approaches are described in Chapter 2.

Eliminating this waste also involves improving each process so there is little or no work-in-process inventory waiting between individual operations. This aspect of just-in-time is described in Chapter 3.

TAKE FIVE

Take five minutes to think about these questions and to write down your answers:

- What problems does inventory cause in your plant?
- What problems does inventory hide in your plant?

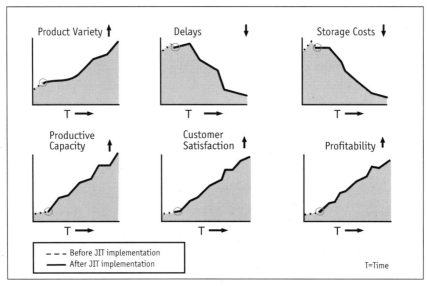

Figure 1-6. Benefits of Just-in-Time

The Benefits of Just-in-Time for Companies

Key Point

Just-in-time helps a company stay competitive by serving its customers better and reducing costs (see Figure 1-6). JIT gives customers the product variety they want. They can get the quantity they need quickly, without paying extra for small runs. A company that can serve its customers this way is likely to be profitable, and flexible enough to change as customer needs change.

BACKGROUND
INFO

In the past, companies simply passed costs on to the customer. The pricing formula was

Cost + Profit = Price

In today's markets, customers insist on a competitive price. This means companies must reduce costs to make profits:

Price − Cost = Profit

Key Point

Just-in-time manufacturing methods also shorten the production lead time. In addition to pleasing the customer, this gives the company an earlier return on its investment of resources in the product.

Key Point

What's more, *a company that implements JIT will discover manufacturing capacity that was hidden in waste.* Just-in-time frees equipment, materials, energy, and employee time—resources that can be redirected to produce other products customers want.

Key Point

Just-in-time manufacturing also promotes continuous improvement. For example, to reduce the safety stock of extra inventory, the company must address the causes of defects and downtime. As problems are solved, delays, rework, and other wastes are removed. Cost saving is one result, but just as important is the competitive edge gained from a high-quality process. Customers expect consistent top quality, and the JIT approach motivates manufacturers to improve products and processes.

The Benefits of JIT for You

Key Point

Implementing just-in-time also benefits you as a company employee. First, *just-in-time supports job security by strengthening the company's competitiveness.* In addition, it also makes daily production work go smoother by

- Removing the clutter of excess work-in-process inventory (WIP)
- Reducing transport and unnecessary handling of work-in-process
- Speeding up machine setups
- Addressing causes of defects and machine problems that cause delays

Key Point

In the course of a just-in-time implementation in your company, you may be asked to learn to perform other operations so that you can substitute for someone or run several pieces of equipment in sequence. This improves your skills and flexibility, and it may change how you think about your role in the company. It is important to recognize that *learning about and participating in a JIT transformation ultimately will make you more employable* by your company, or by any company that hopes to stay at the top in the coming decades.

TAKE FIVE

Take five minutes to think about these questions and to write down your answers:

- Based on what you know so far about JIT, can you see how it might benefit your company? If so, how?
- Can you see how JIT might benefit you? If so, how?

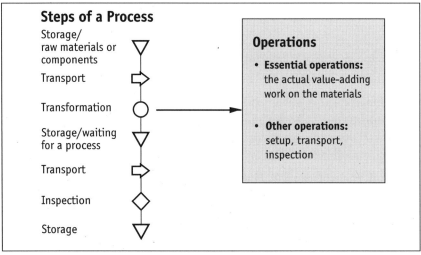

Figure 1-7. Process and Operations

Understanding Processes and Operations

Before we look in detail at the elements of just-in-time, it is important to define a few key terms and concepts.

Processes

Key Term

A *process* is a continuous flow in which raw materials are converted to finished products in a series of operations. The focus of a process is the path of the materials as they are transformed into something to sell.

Manufacturing processes have four basic types of operations or phases:

- **Transformation**: assembly, disassembly, alteration of shape or quality

- **Inspection**: comparison with a standard

- **Transport**: change of location

- **Storage**: a period when no work, transport, or inspection is happening

Materials and parts often go through several of these phases during the manufacturing process. However, only transformation adds value to the product; the other phases should be eliminated or streamlined. The left side of Figure 1-7 shows a typical sequence of process phases.

Operations

Key Term

An *operation*, by contrast, is any action performed by workers or machines on the raw materials, work-in-process, or finished products. The focus of an operation is the specific activity performed.

Key Point

Manufacturing production is thus a network of operations and processes. Referring again to Figure 1-7, each phase of the manufacturing process has one or more corresponding operations. These operations include setup operations as well as essential operations such as machining or assembly work.

Improving Processes as Well as Operations

Since operations involve actions performed on materials or parts, operational improvements often focus on the way actions are carried out. Improving operations, then, might involve adjusting handtool positions to reduce operator fatigue, for example.

Key Point

To improve production, however, it is not enough to improve operations. In implementing just-in-time, a company must also improve its processes. Process improvements actually eliminate or reduce non-value-adding operations that hold up the flow between transformation operations. This means finding ways to reduce delays, storage, transport, mistakes, defects, and other situations that stop the flow.

In just-in-time, materials and WIP pass smoothly through the process, ideally one piece at a time. The rest of this book describes the mechanics of just-in-time and the types of waste-eliminating process and operation improvements that make this smooth flow possible.

TAKE FIVE

Take five minutes to think about these questions and to write down your answers:

- What kind of processes happen in your work area?
- What kind of operations do you perform in your daily work?

11

In Conclusion

SUMMARY

Just-in-time (often called JIT for short) is a manufacturing approach that enables a company to produce the products its customers want, when they want them, and in the amount they want. Implementing JIT often means a new way of controlling the production schedule, a new equipment layout, and new roles for operators.

JIT manufacturing helps companies become more competitive by producing the variety of products customers want while keeping costs low, quality high, and lead time minimal. It does this by eliminating waste in the manufacturing process.

Waste is any element of the manufacturing process that adds cost without adding value to the product. Waste costs money, extends the production lead time, and ties up company resources that could be used productively.

Overproduction occurs when companies create products or work-in-process (WIP) for which they do not currently have orders. It is one of the worst forms of waste, because it generates excess inventory. Large lot production is a leading cause of overproduction.

Inventory is an accumulation of products, WIP, or materials at any stage of the process. Many companies use extra inventory to cover for problems. But when safety stock exists, people are not motivated to make improvements.

Inventory also causes other wastes, including transport, storage, damage, and delay. It also ties up people, equipment, materials, and energy that could be used for more productive work.

Inventory wastes affect every production process that depends on a previous process for materials or parts. To eliminate this waste, companies use just-in-time manufacturing methods to build and deliver just the inventory the customer needs, when needed, in the amount needed.

Just-in-time helps a company stay competitive by serving its customers better and reducing costs. In the past, companies passed costs on to the customer:

Cost + Profit = Price

Today customers insist on a competitive price, so companies must reduce costs to make profits:

Price – Cost = Profit

Just-in-time manufacturing methods also benefit companies by shortening production lead time, freeing wasted capacity in equipment, materials, energy, and employee time, and promoting continuous improvement of the manufacturing process.

Just-in-time benefits employees by strengthening the company's competitiveness, which supports job security. It also makes daily production work go smoother by eliminating various wastes that cause problems.

Also, in a just-in-time implementation you may learn to perform other operations so that you can substitute for someone or run several pieces of equipment in sequence. This improves your skills and flexibility, and it may change how you think about your role in the company.

A manufacturing process is a continuous flow in which raw materials are converted to finished products in a series of operations. The focus of a process is the path of the materials as they are transformed into something to sell. An operation, by contrast, is any action performed by workers or machines on the raw materials, work-in-process, or finished products. The focus of an operation is the specific activity performed.

Manufacturing production is a network of operations and processes. In implementing just-in-time, a company improves processes as well as operations. Process improvements include finding ways to reduce delays, storage, transport, mistakes, defects, and other situations that stop the flow.

REFLECTIONS

Now that you have completed this chapter, take five minutes to think about these questions and to write down your answers:

- What did you learn from reading this chapter that stands out as particularly useful or interesting?

- Do you have any questions about the topics presented in this chapter? If so, what are they?

- What additional information do you need to fully understand the ideas presented in this chapter?

Chapter 2

Basic Concepts of Just-in-Time

Figure 2-1. Basic Concepts of Just-in-Time

This chapter introduces key mechanical concepts that define a just-in-time manufacturing system. Bear in mind that this is a general overview, and that companies may implement these concepts in different ways. For more information about these concepts see the resources listed on pages 66–69.

Leveled Production and Sequencing

Leveled production is a way of scheduling daily production of different types of products in a sequence that evens out the peaks and valleys in the quantities produced. Also called load smoothing or load leveling, leveled production enables companies to supply the variety customers want without building up inventory.

In traditional mass production, the company makes different products in large lots, one type at a time. If a customer wants Product B while the company is making Product A, the customer has to wait. If customers do not purchase the entire lot of Product A right away, part of it becomes inventory and generates the kinds of waste described in Chapter 1. And a shift in customer needs may mean that the company has already made too much of something, or that people and machines must work overtime to produce enough.

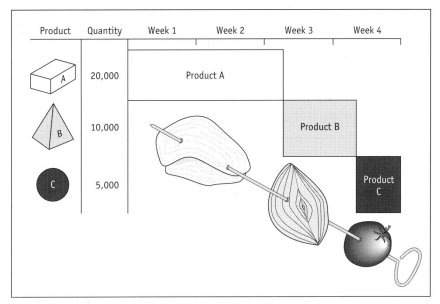

Product	Quantity	Week 1	Week 2	Week 3	Week 4
A	20,000		Product A		
B	10,000			Product B	
C	5,000				Product C

Figure 2-2. Shish-Kebab Production

Key Point

Leveled production, in contrast, allows companies to build the variety desired by customers in a smooth, mixed sequence that minimizes inventory and delays. It also handles minor shifts in projected demand more easily than mass production, by spreading increases or decreases gradually over production for a number of days.

Example

The following example illustrates how leveled production differs from the mass production approach. For this example, assume estimated monthly customer orders of 35,000 units in three different types: 20,000 of product A, 10,000 of product B, and 5,000 of product C.

A Shish-Kebab Production Schedule

Key Term

A mass production company might handle these requirements by making a monthly schedule for building all of product A in a large lot during the first part of the month, then all of product B, followed by all of product C (see Figure 2-2). This large-lot approach is sometimes called *shish-kebab production* because different product types move through the process in chunks, like food on a skewer.

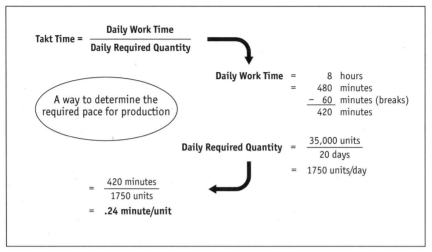

Figure 2-3. Takt Time

A Leveled Production Schedule

Key Point

In *leveled production, the final process first determines how many of each type of product must be made each day to meet customer requirements.* Then, instead of building the different types in lots, the final process uses a daily schedule that evenly mixes the required amounts of various product types in a smooth, repeating sequence.

Takt Time

Key Term

The key to this daily schedule is a calculation called takt time. *Takt time* is the rate at which each product needs to be completed to meet customer requirements. It is the beat or pulse at which each item leaves the process.

Takt time is expressed in minutes (or fraction of minutes) per part. To determine the average takt time for the final process, divide the total daily work time by the quantity of products required each day (see Figure 2-3).

Let's use a daily work time of 420 minutes (8 hours minus 1 hour for breaks and other activities). Assuming 20 work days each month, the daily quantity required would be 35,000 units divided by 20, or 1,750 units. The average takt time for all three product types is 420 divided by 1,750, or 0.24 minute per unit. This means that one product unit should be completed about four times each minute.

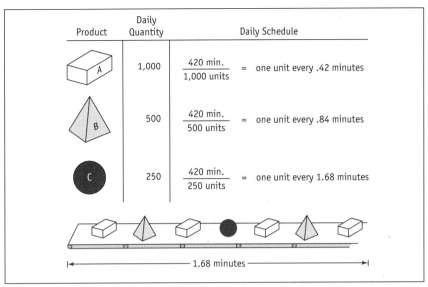

Figure 2-4. Leveled Production Sequence

Production Sequence

To determine a smooth, repeating pattern for making the required amounts of each product type, we calculate the takt time for the daily quantity of each type. As Figure 2-4 shows, one unit of product A should be made every 0.42 minute, with a unit of product B every 0.84 minute, and a unit of product C every 1.68 minutes. To level the production, during the time between units of product C —1.68 minutes—four units of product A need to be made, and two units of product B. This can be turned into a repeating production pattern, as shown in the figure.

To succeed at using leveled production to build products in a mixed sequence, a company must reduce the time required for changeover operations. Chapter 4 outlines an approach for shortening changeover time.

TAKE FIVE

Take five minutes to think about these questions and to write down your answers:

- Do you think your company's production schedule is closer to shish-kebab production or to leveled production?
- What would the average takt time be for the quantity of products your company produces each day?

Figure 2-5. Kanban and the Pull System

Kanban Systems

In a just-in-time system, coordinating the production and movement of parts and components between processes is critical in avoiding excess or shortages. To achieve this coordination, many companies use a system called kanban. The word *kanban* means "card" or "signboard." A kanban system uses cards or other devices as visual signals to control the flow and production of materials (see Figure 2-5).

Key Term

Kanban is a mechanism for managing a "pull" production system. *In a pull system, a process makes more parts only when the next process withdraws parts*—in effect "pulling" the parts from the earlier process when needed. The pull begins with the leveled production schedule for the final process, which is based on actual or expected customer orders. The final process uses kanban to pull needed parts from the previous process, which pulls from the process before it, and so on.

Key Point

In contrast, *the "push" system often used in large-lot production makes parts according to a predetermined schedule for each process*. It will continue to push parts forward on this schedule even when customers do not order them. The push approach often results in wasteful excess inventory.

Key Point

Part Number	Description		Part Number
2347	Mach base		2347
Outbound Stock Area	Inbound Stock Area		Description
G5	A6		Mach base
Container Type	Items/Container		
2T	30		

Move Kanban

Container	Items	Outbound Stock Area
2T	30	G5

Production Kanban

Supplier	ABC	Part Number
Container	Items	2347
2T	30	Description
		Mach base
Bar Code		Delivery Location
		Q7

Supplier Kanban

Figure 2-6. Types of Kanban

Types of Kanban

A typical kanban system uses three main types of kanban cards or devices:

Key Terms

- **Move kanban:** authorizes a process to get parts from the previous process

- **Production kanban:** authorizes the previous process to produce more parts

- **Supplier kanban:** authorizes an outside supplier to deliver more parts

Figure 2-6 shows typical information on these types of kanban. The next several pages give a simple explanation of how the three types of kanban are used to control production. To avoid confusion, we will call the later process "Process 2" and the earlier process that supplies it "Process 1."

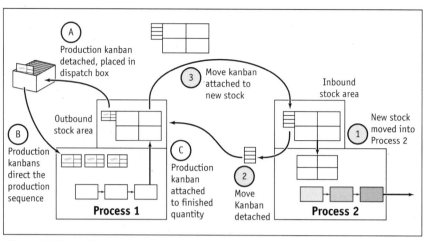

Figure 2-7. How a Kanban System Works

Move Kanban

Example

Each process has an inbound and an outbound stock area. The inbound area holds containers or pallets that contain a small, fixed quantity of materials, parts, or subassemblies used in the process. The outbound area holds the completed output from the process.

Each container in the inbound area has a move kanban attached to it. When Process 2 begins to consume the contents of a container (see 1 in Figure 2-7), the move kanban is taken off the container and brought to the outbound stock area of Process 1 (see 2 in figure). There the move kanban is attached to a new, full container, which is taken back to the inbound stock area of Process 2, ready for use (see 3 in figure).

Production Kanban

Example

A production kanban is attached to every container in the out-bound stock area at Process 1. When Process 2 comes to remove a container of parts, the production kanban is taken off and put in a dispatch box for Process 1 (see A in Figure 2-7). Since Process 1 may make different parts for several other processes, it builds the new parts in the order in which the kanban are placed in the box (see B in figure). When a container is filled with a certain number of parts, the production kanban is attached to it and it is placed in the outbound stock area ready for withdrawal by Process 2 (see C in figure).

Supplier Kanban

Example

Some parts are made by outside suppliers rather than by in-house processes. In this case, a supplier kanban is used in place of a move kanban. It is attached to a full container in the inbound area of the later process. When the process begins consuming that container, the supplier kanban is removed and sent to the outside supplier for replenishment.

TAKE FIVE

Take five minutes to think about these questions and to write down your answers:

- Do you think your company currently uses a push system or a pull system?
- What issues do you see with the way parts production is scheduled at your plant?

Basic Rules of Kanban

Seven basic rules must be followed for successful use of kanban:

1. *The later process goes to the previous process to withdraw only what it needs.* (In some companies, parts and materials are moved between processes by independent handlers. In this case, the handler brings materials from Process 1 only when Process 2 provides a move kanban to authorize the transfer.)

2. *The previous process makes only the quantity needed to replace what was removed by the later process* (or the handler). This quantity is indicated on the kanban.

3. *Defects are never sent to the next process.* This means that production is stopped until the problems are corrected. In a low-inventory production system, this motivates preventive improvements such as mistake-proofing and autonomation (described in Chapters 3 and 4).

4. *A kanban must always accompany products on the line.* Since only a certain number of kanban exist, they serve as a visual control of the amount of inventory allowed in the work area.

5. *Production quantities must be leveled to avoid fluctuation and eliminate waste.* Spreading the quantity evenly over time helps assure a smooth flow between processes.

6. *Use kanban to fine-tune the schedule.* Since production happens when instructed by the kanban, small increases or decreases in the amount to be produced can be handled easily by changing how often kanban are transferred between processes. Kanban systems are not well suited to handle large fluctuations in customer demand.

7. *Stabilize, rationalize, and simplify the process.* Like rule 3, this rule is about improvement—in this case, improving the process to avoid waste and unpredictability.

Improve the Process First

Key Point

Keep in mind that kanban is just a system for controlling inventory. *If the processes themselves have not been improved to eliminate waste such as excess WIP, walking, conveyance, downtime, and defects, kanban will not work.* Chapters 3 and 4 describe key process improvement and standardization techniques that support the use of kanban for just-in-time.

In Conclusion

SUMMARY

Leveled production is a way of scheduling daily production of different types of products in a sequence that evens out peaks and valleys in the quantities produced. Leveled production (also called load smoothing or load leveling) enables companies to supply the variety customers want without building up inventory.

In traditional mass production, different products are made in large lots, one type at a time. This approach is sometimes called shish-kebab production, because different product types move through the process in chunks, like food on a skewer. If a customer wants Product B while the company is making Product A, the customer has to wait. If customers do not purchase the entire lot of Product A right away, part of it becomes inventory.

Leveled production, in contrast, allows companies to build the variety desired by customers in a smooth, mixed sequence that minimizes inventory and delays. In leveled production, the final process first determines how many of each type of product must be made each day to meet customer requirements. Then, instead of building the different types in lots, the final process uses a daily schedule that evenly mixes the required amounts of various product types in a smooth, repeating sequence.

The key to this daily schedule is a calculation called takt time — the rate at which each product needs to be completed to meet customer requirements. Expressed in minutes (or fraction of minutes) per part, it is the beat or pulse at which each item leaves the process.

To determine a smooth, repeating pattern for making the required amounts of each product type, we calculate the takt time for the daily quantity of each type.

Coordinating the production and movement of parts and components between processes is critical in avoiding excess or shortages. To achieve this coordination, many companies use a system called kanban. The word kanban means "card" or "sign board." A kanban system uses cards or other devices as visual signals to control the flow and production of materials.

Kanban is a mechanism for managing a "pull" production system. In a pull system, a process makes more parts only when the next process pulls parts. The pull begins with the leveled production schedule for the final process, which is based on actual or expected customer orders. The final process uses kanban to pull needed parts from the previous process, which pulls from the process before it, and so on.

In contrast, the "push" system makes parts according to a predetermined schedule for each process. It pushes parts forward on this schedule whether or not there are orders, which often results in wasteful excess inventory.

A typical kanban system uses three main types of kanban cards or devices:

- **Move kanban:** authorizes a process to get parts from the previous process
- **Production kanban:** authorizes the previous process to produce more parts
- **Supplier kanban:** authorizes an outside supplier to deliver more parts

There are seven basic rules for successful use of kanban:

1. The later process goes to the previous process to withdraw only what it needs.

2. The previous process makes only the quantity needed to replace what was removed by the later process.

3. Defects are never sent to the next process.

4. A kanban must always accompany products on the line.

5. Production quantities must be leveled to avoid fluctuation and eliminate waste.

6. Use kanban to fine-tune the schedule.

7. Stabilize, rationalize, and simplify the process.

Successful use of kanban requires process improvements to eliminate waste and excess inventory.

REFLECTIONS

Now that you have completed this chapter, take five minutes to think about these questions and to write down your answers:

• What did you learn from reading this chapter that stands out as particularly useful or interesting?

• Do you have any questions about the topics presented in this chapter? If so, what are they?

• What additional information do you need to fully understand the ideas presented in this chapter?

Chapter 3

Process Improvement and Standardization

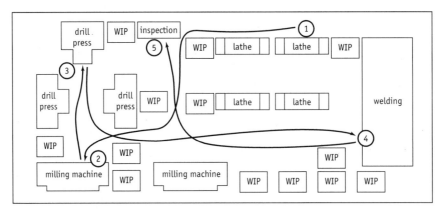

Figure 3-1. An Operation-Based Layout

Wastes Resulting from Operation-Based Layouts

Most manufacturing processes contain so much waste that just-in-time cannot work until improvements are made. Process improvements to eliminate waste often include changes in the equipment layout on the plant floor.

Many companies group the production equipment according to the type of operation performed. For example, all the drill presses may be located near each other (see Figure 3-1). Parts are often processed in large lots to avoid the need for changeovers. *This operation-based layout leads to several kinds of waste*:

Key Point

- **Conveyance:** Most processes include operations on several different types of equipment. To reach the next step, components often must travel to another equipment area (see Figure 3-1). This travel requires equipment (forklifts or conveyors), energy, and sometimes people, but it adds no value to the product.

- **Wasted space:** Large machines, large lots of WIP, and conveyance equipment all take up space that could be used more effectively.

- **Lot delays:** Processing parts in lots or batches causes delay because the first item in the lot doesn't move to the next step until the last item in the lot is processed.

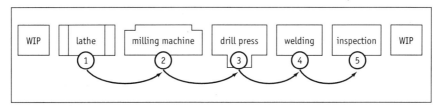

Figure 3-2. A Process-Based Layout

Benefits of a Process Flow Layout

Key Point

Positioning manufacturing equipment closely together in the order of the processing steps reduces waste and improves the flow in several ways. For one thing, *placing the machines for each step side by side eliminates much of the waste of conveying work-in-process long distances* (see Figure 3-2).

Key Point

Key Term

What's more, *a process-based layout allows materials and parts to flow through the process steps in small batches or even one by one, without large amounts of WIP between steps*. This approach, called *flow manufacturing*, not only saves space, but also eliminates lot delays so that parts flow through the process quicker.

> ## TAKE FIVE
>
> Take five minutes to think about these questions and to write down your answers:
>
> • How is equipment arranged in your workplace?
> • Do you think this layout has waste in it? If so, what kinds?

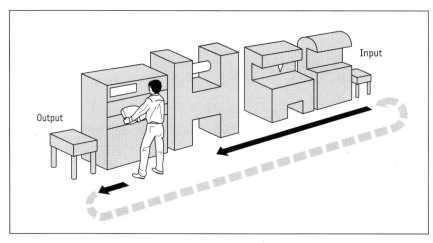

Figure 3-3. Operating Multiple Machines in a Process-Based Layout

Multi-Machine Operation

A process-based equipment layout changes the relationship between people and machines and often requires some changes in operating assignments. In an operation-based layout, for example, all the presses are located together and one person may run several similar machines. However, when the machines are rearranged in a process sequence, each press may become part of a different processing line. In that situation, it is probably not economical to have one press operator for each individual process. What's more, if the equipment is automated, most of the operator's time would be spent watching it run. This is a huge waste of human potential.

These wastes are avoided by cross-training people to operate several different machines in the process. When an operator is trained on several machines, he or she is able to step into any position to respond to changes in the production pattern. *With automation, operators can manage the flow of work through a series of machines in the process, sometimes handling one workpiece at a time* (see Figure 3-3). For example, while the step 1 machine is processing the second piece, the operator can be setting up the first piece on the step 2 equipment, and so on.

Key Point

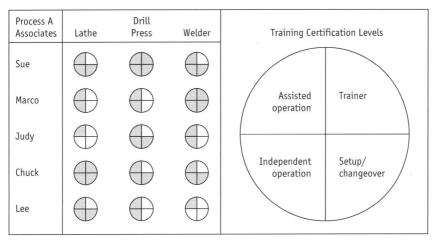

Figure 3-4. A Cross-Training Chart

Cross-Training

Key Point

Cross-training enables employees to perform different functions within a process and lets teams take full responsibility for their processes. This versatility makes employees more valuable to their teams and to their companies. Cross-training is a source of employee pride in many workplaces. Visual display charts are often used to recognize people's skill attainment in a public way (see Figure 3-4).

Moving with the Process

Key Point

To run several machines in sequence, an operator needs to work standing up rather than sitting down. Flow manufacturing implies movement of the parts through the process. To assist this flow, people need to stand and walk. Working while standing also enables people to respond more quickly if machine problems occur.

TAKE FIVE

Take five minutes to think about these questions and to write down your answers:

• Do operators at your company run different kinds of machines? If not, what would need to happen to make this possible?

• Do operators run more than one machine? If not, what would need to happen to make this possible?

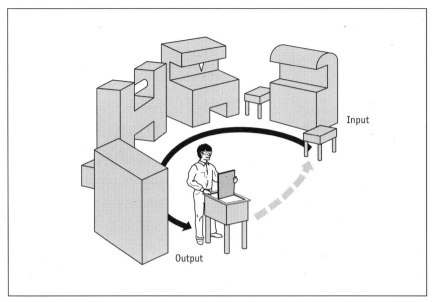

Figure 3-5. A U-Shaped Cell Layout

U-Shaped Cells

It is possible to implement flow manufacturing with the equipment for each operation arranged in a straight line. However, when the operator finishes the last step of the process, he or she must walk back to the first step to start again. This walking is waste that adds no value to the product.

Key Term

Key Point

To eliminate this waste, flow manufacturing often uses an equipment arrangement called a U-shaped cell. In a *U-shaped cell*, the equipment is placed in process sequence in a horseshoe pattern. In this layout, *the last processing step is very close to the first step, so the operator is not walking as far to begin the next cycle* (see Figure 3-5).

Small, Flexible Machines

Key Point

A just-in-time process may use equipment different from that used in large-lot production. *Flow manufacturing works best with machines that are smaller and often slower than large-lot equipment.*

Smaller machines can be used for flow manufacturing because the goal is to process one or a few items at a time, instead of large batches. Smaller machines save space. Placing them close together reduces the walking distance and leaves no space for excess WIP to accumulate.

Slower machines are appropriate for flow manufacturing because the objective is not to produce large lots of WIP quickly. Instead, machines produce one piece at a time at a speed determined by customer requirements.

Key Point

Machines for flow manufacturing also need to be flexible. To maximize their usefulness, they must be easy to set up quickly so they can be used to make a greater variety of products during a single shift. (See Chapter 4 for more about quick changeover.)

Flexible may also mean movable. Mounting smaller machines on casters makes it possible to move them to other locations as needed, or to experiment with new production layouts.

Another benefit of using smaller machines for flow manufacturing is that they generally are less expensive to purchase and easier to operate and maintain.

TAKE FIVE

Take five minutes to think about these questions and to write down your answers:

- How does a U-shaped equipment layout eliminate waste?
- Do you think the equipment in your area is better suited to large-lot production or to flow manufacturing? Why?

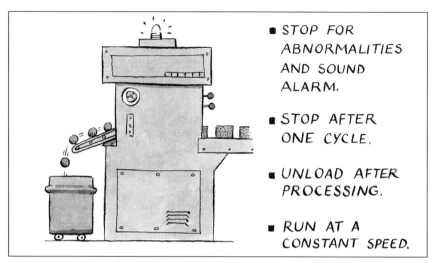

STOP FOR ABNORMALITIES AND SOUND ALARM.

STOP AFTER ONE CYCLE.

UNLOAD AFTER PROCESSING.

RUN AT A CONSTANT SPEED.

Figure 3-6. Typical Features of Autonomation

Autonomation

Key Term

Another characteristic of the equipment used in just-in-time manufacturing is autonomation (also called *jidoka*). *Autonomation* is an approach to automation that gives equipment "intelligence" so people don't have to monitor automatic operation.

Key Point

"Autonomated" machines are semi-automatic machines that autonomously (independently) support continuous flow processing. *They stop and signal when a cycle is complete or when defects occur* (see Figure 3-6). Although such machines are often loaded in the process sequence by operators, they also may unload automatically after processing.

Many companies invest in automated equipment so people don't have to perform difficult, dangerous, or repetitive work. At a lot of factories, however, people still watch the automated equipment "just in case" something goes wrong. Autonomation frees people from this non-value-adding role by modifying machines so they can run with little supervision.

Key Term

The function of stopping for problems is also a key element of the mistake-proofing approach called *poka-yoke*. Poka-yoke systems are described further in Chapter 4.

The technology required for autonomation is often very simple. It is usually not expensive to modify existing machines to perform this way.

When people don't have to watch the machine to spot problems or to catch the output, they have time to perform more value-adding work, such as operating several machines in sequence or planning and implementing new ideas for improving the work flow.

TAKE FIVE

Take five minutes to think about these questions and to write down your answers:

• Do people in your work area monitor automated equipment?
• If so, what are some of the things they watch for?

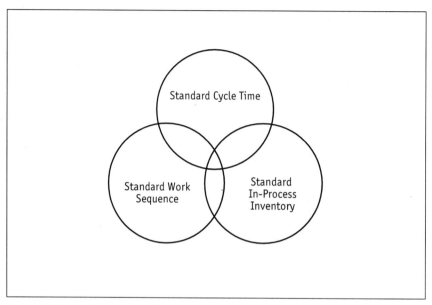

Figure 3-7. Three Components of Standard Work

Standard Work

As you improve your process and the operations within it, it is important to standardize the way the work is done. Standard processes are essential for just-in-time delivery of component parts. In a pull system, later processes count on the ability of earlier processes to make or supply a certain quantity of parts at a certain time, given a certain lead time. If the previous process is unpredictable, just-in-time delivery can't happen.

Key Point

To establish predictability in processing cycles, each process determines its standard work (also called standard operations). As Figure 3-7 shows, standard work has three parts:

- Standard cycle time

- Standard work sequence

- Standard in-process inventory (WIP)

Figure 3-8. Cycle Time

Standard Cycle Time

Key Term

Cycle time is the actual time required to process one part. Cycle time is determined by timing the operations in a process from start to finish, including machine processing time as well as manual work, walking, waiting, and inspection (see Figure 3-8). Operations are usually clocked several times; the average time is used as the current standard cycle time.

Key Point

Process cycle time determines whether a process is capable of producing the quantity required by the next process at the required time. The time requirements of each process are ultimately controlled by the takt time for the final process. If a process makes parts faster than needed, excess inventory will be created unless production is strictly controlled by kanban or other means. It is better to remain idle; idleness is a visual indicator of excess capacity that could be used another way.

On the other hand, if the cycle time is slower than needed, shortages will delay the next process. Process improvements may be needed to avoid delays, or additional people or machines may be used to ensure a smooth flow.

Figure 3-9. The Need for a Standard Work Sequence

Standard Work Sequence

Key Point

It is not possible to have a consistent cycle time without a consistent work sequence and method (see Figure 3-9). *Documenting the steps carried out by people and machines helps ensure that work is done the same best way each time.* This standardization is also important for top-quality products and a safe workplace.

Standard In-Process Inventory

Key Point

To standardize the work that takes place in a process, you also must standardize the minimum quantity of parts or materials needed to complete one processing cycle and allow the cycle to continue. *The goal to aim for is one-piece flow of workpieces through the process.* This means that individual pieces of WIP move directly from one operation to the next rather than piling up between operations.

TAKE FIVE

Take five minutes to think about these questions and to write down your answers:

• Do you know the cycle time for the processes in your work area?
• Is work done using a consistent sequence and method?
• How much WIP is in your work area at any given time?

Standard Work Forms

Companies document their standard work on a set of forms. Companies may use different names for these forms or combine them in different ways, but the functions are essentially similar. Commonly used forms include the following:

Key Terms

• **Process Capacity Table** (see Figure 3-10): This form records the operator and machine time currently required for each step of the process, as well as the tool changeover time. It helps indicate bottlenecks in the process.

• **Standard Work Combination Sheet** (see Figure 3-11): This form charts the relationship between machine operation time and human work time in a process.

• **Standard Work Sheet** (see Figure 3-12): This form documents the current standard sequence of processing steps and the equipment layout for this sequence. Some companies also include the worker and machine times for each step.

	Approval stamps	**Process Capacity Table**					Part no.		Type	RY	Entered by	ST
							Part name	6" pinion	Quantity	1	Creation date	1/17

Process	Process name	Serial no.	Manual operation time (A)		Basic times				Blades and bits		Per unit retooling time F = E + D	Total time per unit G = C + F	Production capacity I/G	Graph time
					Auto feed time (B)		Completion time C = A + B		Retooling amount (D)	Retooling time (E)				Manual work - - - - Auto feed ————
			Min.	Sec.	Min.	Sec.	Min.	Sec.						
1	Pick up raw materials	—		1		—		1	—	—	—	1	—	
2	Gear teeth cutting	A01		4		35		39	400	2'10"	0.3"	39.3	717	4"+ - - -35"- - -⌐
3	Gear teeth surface fin.	A02		6		15		21	1,000	2'00"	0.1"	21.1	1,336	6"+ _15"_ ⌐
4	Forward gear surface fin.	A03		7		38		45	400	3'00"	0.5"	45.5	619	7"+ - - -38"- - -⌐
5	Reverse gear surface fin.	A04		5		28		33	400	2'30"	0.4"	33.4	844	5"+ _28"_ - -⌐
6	Pin width measurement	B01		8		5		13	—	—		13	259	8"+ 5"⌐
7	Store finished workpiece	—		1		—		1	—	—	—	1	—	

Figure 3-10. Process Capacity Table

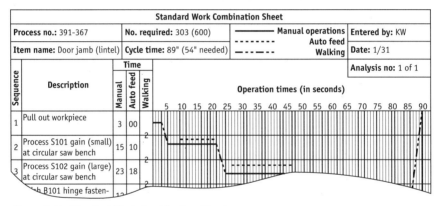

Figure 3-11. Standard Work Combination Sheet

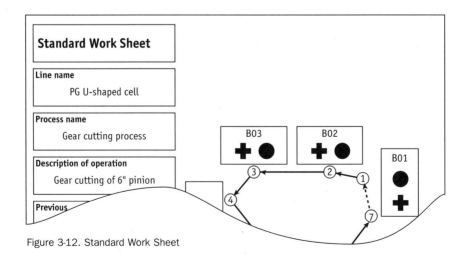

Figure 3-12. Standard Work Sheet

Figure 3-13. Standards as the Baseline for Improvement

The Foundation for Continuous Improvement

Unlike a time or motion study, standard work is developed by the people who do the work. Standardization helps the people in the workplace understand when the process is out of standard and sets the stage for improvement.

Key Point

It is important to remember that developing standard work is only the beginning. *Standardization is the first step in improvement* (see Figure 3-13). Only by doing work the same way each time can you know whether trial changes are having the desired result. Standard work defines the method used by everyone—but it is also a "living" standard that should be continuously improving.

TAKE FIVE

Take five minutes to think about this question and to write down your answer:

• How are standards for processes and operations currently developed in your workplace?

In Conclusion

SUMMARY

Most manufacturing processes contain so much waste that just-in-time cannot work until improvements are made. Process improvements to eliminate waste often include changes in the equipment layout on the plant floor.

Positioning manufacturing equipment closely together in the order of the processing steps reduces waste and improves the flow. Placing the machines for each step side by side eliminates much of the waste of conveying work-in-process long distances. Also, a process-based layout allows materials and parts to flow through the process in small batches without large amounts of WIP between steps.

A process-based equipment layout changes the relationship between people and machines and often requires some changes in operating assignments. When the machines are rearranged in a process sequence, it is probably not economical to have one press operator for each individual process. Having people watch automated machines is also a huge waste of human potential. Automation should allow operators to manage the flow of work through a series of machines in the process. Cross-training enables employees to perform different functions within a process and lets teams take full responsibility for their processes.

To run several machines in sequence, an operator needs to work standing up rather than sitting down. Flow manufacturing implies movement of the parts through the process. To assist this flow, people need to stand and walk. Working while standing also enables people to respond more quickly if machine problems occur.

Flow manufacturing often uses an equipment arrangement called a U-shaped cell in which the equipment is placed in process sequence in a horseshoe pattern. In this layout, the last step is very close to the first step, so the operator does not have to walk far to begin the next cycle.

Flow manufacturing works best with machines that are smaller and often slower than large-lot equipment. Smaller machines save space, and placing them close together reduces the walking distance and leaves no space for excess WIP to accumulate. Slower machines avoid overproduction by making one piece at a time at a speed determined by customer requirements.

Autonomation is an approach to automation that gives equipment "intelligence" so people don't have to monitor automatic operation. "Autonomated" machines stop and signal when a cycle is complete or when defects occur. They also may unload automatically after processing, or catch errors that could cause defects.

While improving the process, it is important to standardize the way work is done. In a pull system, later processes count on the ability of earlier processes to make or supply a certain quantity of parts at a certain time, given a certain lead time. To establish this predictability in processing cycles, each process determines its standard work. Standard work has three components:

- Standard cycle time (the actual time required to process one part)
- Standard work sequence
- Standard in-process inventory (WIP)

Companies document their standard operations on a set of forms:

- Process Capacity Table
- Standard Work Combination Sheet
- Standard Work Sheet

Unlike a time or motion study, standard work is developed by the people who do the work. Standardization helps the people in the workplace understand when the process is out of standard and sets the stage for improvement. Standard work is a "living" standard that should be continuously improving.

REFLECTIONS

Now that you have completed this chapter, take five minutes to think about these questions and to write down your answers:

• What did you learn from reading this chapter that stands out as particularly useful or interesting?

• Do you have any questions about the topics presented in this chapter? If so, what are they?

• What additional information do you need to fully understand the ideas presented in this chapter?

Chapter 4

Support Techniques for Just-in-Time

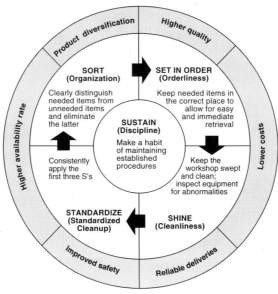

Figure 4-1. The 5S System

This chapter describes several important techniques that support the smooth flow required for just-in-time manufacturing. Additional information is available in the resources listed on pages 66–69.

The 5S System for Workplace Organization and Standardization

The just-in-time approach cannot succeed in a workplace that is cluttered, disorganized, or dirty. Poor workplace conditions give rise to all sorts of waste, including extra motion to avoid obstacles, time spent searching for needed items, and delays due to quality defects, equipment breakdowns, and accidents.

Key Point

Establishing good basic workplace conditions is an essential first step in any shopfloor improvement program. Many companies use the 5S system to improve and standardize the physical condition of their work areas. The *5S system* is a set of five basic principles with names beginning with S:

Key Term

- Sort
- Set in Order
- Shine
- Standardize
- Sustain

Key Terms

Sort: Teams begin by sorting out and removing items that are not needed in the work area. They use a technique called Red Tagging to identify unneeded items and manage their disposition.

Set in Order: Next, teams determine appropriate locations for the items they do need. After relocating the items, they apply temporary lines, labels, and signboards to indicate the new positions. The main idea is, "A place for everything, and everything in its place."

Shine: The third S involves a top to bottom cleaning of the work area, including the equipment. Shine also means inspecting equipment during cleaning to spot early signs of trouble that could lead to defects, breakdowns, or accidents.

Standardize: In the fourth S, people establish the new, improved conditions as a workplace standard. At this stage, visual management methods are adopted to ensure that everyone in the workplace understands and can easily follow the new standards.

Sustain: The final 5S principle uses training and communication to maintain and monitor the improved conditions and to spread 5S activities to other areas of the company.

TAKE FIVE

Take five minutes to think about these questions and to write down your answers:

- Are there physical conditions that get in the way of doing the work in your area?
- What specific conditions would you change to make the work area easier to use?

Figure 4-2. An Andon Board

Visual Management Techniques

Visual management of the production process is an important support for just-in-time. For example, kanban cards or containers are visual management tools that control when materials or parts are made or moved to another process.

Visual management techniques express information in a way that can be understood quickly by everyone.

One form of visual management seen in many just-in-time factories is the andon system. In an *andon system,* individual machines or assembly stations are equipped with call lamps. When a problem occurs, the operator (or the machine itself) turns on the light to call attention. At many plants, overhead andon boards also show the status of several machines or lines to help others locate the problem (see Figure 4-2). Andon lamps and boards are also used to call materials handlers when parts need replenishing.

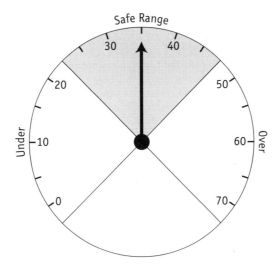

Figure 4-3. A Color Coded Dial Gauge

Key Point

Visual techniques help keep order in the workplace. Lines, labels, and signboards (introduced in the discussion of 5S on page 49) tell everyone, at a glance, where to find things and where to put them away. Using these methods to indicate locations can eliminate a lot of time wasted in searching.

Key Point

Example

Visual information can also help prevent mistakes. Color coding is a form of visual display often used to prevent errors. Shaded red and green "pie slices" on a dial gauge give an instant status reading (see Figure 4-3). Color matching is another approach that helps people use the right tool or assemble the right part.

TAKE FIVE

Take five minutes to think about these questions and to write down your answers:

- Can you find examples of visual displays already used in your workplace?
- Can you think of other ways to use visual methods to reduce waste and errors?

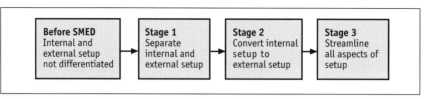

Figure 4-4. The Three Stages of SMED

Quick Changeover Methods for Flexible Lot Sizes

In the past, companies produced in large lots because setting up for a different product took so much time from production that it wasn't economical unless the cost was spread over a large quantity. However, large-lot production often means large inventories and all the problems, wastes, and costs associated with them. Just-in-time manufacturing requires us to process items in small lots, even lots of only one item.

Key Point

To produce economically in smaller lots, a company must learn how to reduce the time required for changeovers. The single-minute exchange of die* (SMED) approach developed by Shigeo Shingo gives a three-stage system for shortening setup time (see Figure 4-4).

Stage 1: Separate Internal Setup from External Setup

Key Terms

Internal setup refers to setup operations that can be done only with the equipment stopped. *External setup* operations can be done while the machine is running. At many companies internal and external setup operations are jumbled together. This means that things that could be done while the machine is running are not done until the machine is stopped.

Stage 1 involves sorting out the external operations so they can be done beforehand. This step alone can reduce setup time by 30 to 50 percent. Typical stage 1 activities include

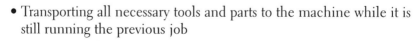
Examples

- Transporting all necessary tools and parts to the machine while it is still running the previous job

- Confirming the function of exchangeable parts before stopping the machine for changeover

---

*Named for the goal of completing changeover within a single-digit number of minutes—9 minutes or less.

Stage 2: Convert Internal Setup to External Setup

The next step is to look again at activities done with the machine stopped and to find ways to do them while the machine is still active. Typical stage 2 improvements include

Examples

- Preparing operating conditions in advance, such as preheating a die mold with a heater instead of using trial shots of molten material
- Using devices that automatically position the parts without measurement

Stage 3: Streamline All Aspects of Setup

This stage chips away at remaining internal setup time in several ways:

Examples

- Using parallel operations, with two or more people working simultaneously
- Using functional clamps instead of nuts and bolts
- Using numerical settings to eliminate trial-and-error adjustments

---

TAKE FIVE

Take five minutes to think about these questions and to write down your answers:

- How long does a typical changeover take in your work area?
- Can you list the changeover steps that should take place while the machine is still running?

Zero Quality Control Elements

1. *Source inspection* to catch errors before they become defects

2. *100 percent inspection* to check every workpiece, not just a sample

3. *Immediate feedback* to shorten the time for corrective action

4. *Poka-yoke* (mistake-proofing) devices to check automatically for abnormalities

Figure 4-5. The Four Elements of ZQC

Zero Defects Through Zero Quality Control

BACKGROUND
INFO

Zero defects is a basic expectation of the customer. In addition to the costs of scrap or rework, even one defect can ruin the company's reputation with the customer who gets it. And in just-in-time manufacturing, there is no extra supply of WIP to replace defects that are "inspected out."

Key Point

The key to zero defects is to detect and prevent abnormal conditions before they can cause defects. Zero quality control (ZQC, or QC for zero defects) is a defect prevention system that uses inspection at the point where it can prevent defects—before the processing takes place.

ZQC combines four basic elements:

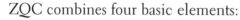

Key Points

1. It uses *source inspection* to catch errors before they become defects.

2. It uses *100 percent inspection* to check every workpiece, not just a sample.

3. It provides *immediate feedback*, thereby shortening the time for corrective action.

4. Because people naturally make mistakes or miss things, ZQC uses *poka-yoke* (mistake-proofing) devices on processing or assembly equipment to check automatically for abnormalities.

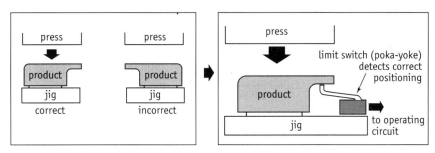

Figure 4-6. A Poka-Yoke Example

Poka-Yoke Systems

Key Term

A *poka-yoke* system uses sensors or other devices to detect errors that could cause defects. The most effective poka-yokes not only sound an alarm (instant feedback) but also stop the process so a defect cannot be made. For example, a limit switch can be positioned so the machine will not start when the workpiece is loaded incorrectly (see Figure 4-6). This prevents operation that would produce a defect.

A nonelectronic poka-yoke example is a jig with an uneven pattern of notches or pins so the workpiece cannot be positioned in it incorrectly.

Key Point

The key to effective mistake-proofing is determining when and where defect-causing conditions arise and then figuring out how to detect or prevent these conditions, every time. Shopfloor people have important knowledge and ideas to share for developing and implementing poka-yoke systems that check every item and give immediate feedback about the problem.

TAKE FIVE

Take five minutes to think about these questions and to write down your answers:

• What kinds of actions or conditions can cause defects to happen in your process? Can you think of ways to "catch" these conditions before defects are made?

Figure 4-7. A Definition of TPM

Total Productive Maintenance for Dependable Equipment

The health of processing and assembly equipment can make or break the JIT implementation effort. Manufacturing just-in-time, without large WIP buffers between processes, requires dependable equipment that will perform as needed, when needed.

Key Term

Total productive maintenance (TPM) is a good way to ensure that equipment is ready when it is needed. *TPM is a comprehensive, companywide approach for reducing equipment-related losses such as downtime, speed reduction, and defects by stabilizing and improving equipment conditions.* The definition in Figure 4-7 describes five key aspects.

Key Point

The TPM framework improves equipment effectiveness through various approaches that involve everyone in the company. Frontline workers, especially, have a key role in the TPM activity called autonomous maintenance.

Autonomous Maintenance

Key Term

Autonomous maintenance refers to activities carried out by operators in cooperation with maintenance staff to help stabilize basic equipment conditions and spot problems early. Autonomous maintenance changes the old view that operators just run machines and maintenance people just fix them. Operators have

Figure 4-8. Autonomous Maintenance Involves Everyone

valuable knowledge and skill that can be used to help keep equipment from breaking down.

Key Point

In autonomous maintenance, operators learn how to clean the equipment they use every day, and how to inspect for trouble signs as they clean (see Figure 4-8). They may also learn basic lubrication routines, or at least how to check for adequate lubrication. They learn simple methods to reduce contamination and keep the equipment cleaner. Ultimately, they learn more about the various operating systems of the equipment and may assist technicians with repairs. Autonomous maintenance training helps operators work as partners with maintenance and engineering to keep equipment working as effectively as possible.

TAKE FIVE

Take five minutes to think about these questions and to write down your answers:

- Who performs basic cleaning and maintenance on the equipment in your work area?
- Do you think autonomous maintenance activities would reduce unplanned downtime in your company? Why or why not?

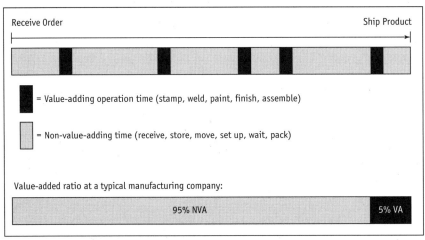

Figure 4-9. The Value-Added Ratio

New Measures of Excellence

Key Point

It is common wisdom that "what gets measured is what gets done." *To support just-in-time, it is crucial to use measures that reinforce the new way of operating.* Reliance on traditional measures such as equipment or labor efficiency may make it hard to change, since efficiency in the traditional sense tends to generate large quantities of inventory.

Performance measures for JIT should not only recognize improvement but also show the remaining waste to be addressed. Here are some examples of performance measures that help motivate people to do the right things:

Key Term

Value-added ratio: This measure indicates how much of the total production lead time is spent in actual processing operations that transform the materials and add value for the customer (see Figure 4-9).

Key Term

Production lead time: Companies track the time elapsed from the order to the shipped product. Shorter lead time is an important competitive advantage. Combining this with the value-added ratio yields insights into phases of production that need to be improved.

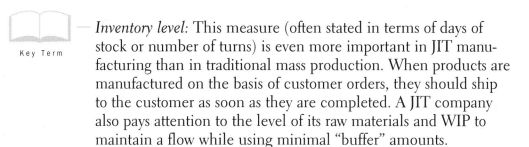

Inventory level: This measure (often stated in terms of days of stock or number of turns) is even more important in JIT manufacturing than in traditional mass production. When products are manufactured on the basis of customer orders, they should ship to the customer as soon as they are completed. A JIT company also pays attention to the level of its raw materials and WIP to maintain a flow while using minimal "buffer" amounts.

Setup time: Quick changeover is critical to flexible use of equipment to produce wide variety in small lots.

Distance moved: This measure tracks the waste of moving WIP between processes. A process-based layout should reduce this transport.

Defect rate: Zero defects is the goal, and not just in final inspection. Tracking defect rates for each process promotes mistake-proofing and machine or method improvements all along the line.

Overall equipment effectiveness (OEE): This is the basic measurement for total productive maintenance. It is a percentage calculated by multiplying the availability rate, the performance efficiency (performance rate), and the quality rate. These three rates are linked directly to specific types of equipment-related losses (wastes) that can be targeted for improvement.

TAKE FIVE

Take five minutes to think about these questions and to write down your answers:

- What kind of measures drive performance at your company?
- What measures do you think are important to promote just-in-time manufacturing? To promote employee morale? To promote customer satisfaction?

In Conclusion

SUMMARY

Establishing good basic workplace conditions is an essential first step in any shopfloor improvement program. Many companies use the 5S system to improve and standardize the physical condition of their work areas. The 5S system sorts and removes unneeded items, determines best locations for needed items, cleans thoroughly, and then establishes standards for maintaining improved conditions.

Visual management of the production process is an important support for just-in-time. Visual management techniques express information in a way that can be understood quickly by everyone. The andon system is a form of visual management that uses lights to alert people to equipment problems. Lines, labels, and signboards can be used to indicate where to find things and where to put them away. Color coding can help prevent mistakes and make information easier to understand.

Quick changeover is essential for manufacturing different product types in small lots. The SMED approach gives a three-stage system for shortening setup:

1. Separate internal setup (activities that require the machine to be stopped) from external setup (activities that can be done while the machine is still running).

2. Convert internal setup to external setup.

3. Streamline all aspects of setup.

The first step alone can reduce setup time by 30 to 50 percent.

Zero defects is also critical for smooth just-in-time production. The key to zero defects is to detect and prevent abnormal conditions before they can cause defects. Zero quality control (ZQC) combines four elements to catch all problems at the error or abnormality stage. One of these elements—the poka-yoke (mistake-proofing) system—uses simple sensors or other devices to check automatically for errors. The most effective poka-yokes not only sound an alarm but also stop the process so a defect cannot be made.

Manufacturing just-in-time, without large WIP buffers between processes, requires dependable equipment that will perform as needed, when needed. Total productive maintenance (TPM) helps ensure that equipment is ready when needed. TPM is a comprehensive, companywide approach for reducing equipment-related losses.

TPM improves equipment effectiveness through approaches that involve everyone in the company. Frontline workers have a key role in the TPM activity called autonomous maintenance—activities carried out by operators in cooperation with maintenance to help stabilize equipment conditions and spot problems early. Autonomous maintenance changes the old view that operators just run machines and maintenance people just fix them.

It is common wisdom that "what gets measured is what gets done." To support just-in-time, it is crucial to use measures that reinforce the new way of operating. Reliance on traditional measures such as equipment or labor efficiency may make it hard to change, since efficiency in the traditional sense tends to generate large quantities of inventory. Performance measures for JIT should not only recognize improvement but also show the remaining waste to be addressed.

REFLECTIONS

Now that you have completed this chapter, take five minutes to think about these questions and to write down your answers:

• What did you learn from reading this chapter that stands out as particularly useful or interesting?

• Do you have any questions about the topics presented in this chapter? If so, what are they?

• What additional information do you need to fully understand the ideas presented in this chapter?

Chapter 5

Reflections and Conclusions

Reflecting on What You've Learned

Key Point

An important part of learning is reflecting on what you've learned. Without this step, learning can't take place effectively. That's why we've asked you at the end of each chapter to reflect on what you've learned. And now that you've reached the end of the book, we'd like to ask you to reflect on what you've learned from the book as a whole.

Take ten minutes to think about the following questions and to write down your answers.

- What did you learn from reading this book that stands out as particularly useful or interesting?

- What ideas, concepts, and techniques have you learned that will be most useful to you during just-in-time implementation? How will they be useful?

- What ideas, concepts, and techniques have you learned that will be least useful during just-in-time implementation? Why won't they be useful?

- Do you have any questions about the just-in-time approach? If so, what are they?

Opportunities for Further Learning

How-to Steps

Here are some ways to learn more about just-in-time manufacturing:

- Find other books, videos, or trainings on this subject. Several are listed on the next pages.

- If your company is already implementing just-in-time, visit other departments or areas to see how they are applying the ideas and approaches you have learned about here.

- Find out how other companies have implemented just-in-time. You can do this by reading magazines and books about JIT and lean manufacturing, and by attending conferences and seminars presented by others.

Conclusions

Just-in-time is more than a series of techniques. It is a fundamental approach for improving the manufacturing process. We hope this book has given you a taste of how and why this approach can be helpful and effective for you in your work.

Additional Resources Related to JIT and Shopfloor Improvement

Books and Videos

Just-in-Time and Lean Manufacturing

Jeffrey Liker, *Becoming Lean: Inside Stories of U.S. Manufacturers* (Productivity Press, 1997)—This book shares powerful first-hand accounts of the complete process of implementing just-in-time and other lean methods.

Japan Management Association, ed., *Kanban and Just-in-Time at Toyota* (Productivity Press, 1986)—This classic overview book describes the underlying concepts and main techniques of the original just-in-time system.

Taiichi Ohno, *Toyota Production System* (Productivity Press, 1988)—This is the story of the first just-in-time system, told by the Toyota vice president who was responsible for implementing it.

Hiroyuki Hirano, *JIT Factory Revolution* (Productivity Press, 1988)—This book of photographs and diagrams gives an excellent overview of the changes involved in implementing just-in-time.

Hiroyuki Hirano, *JIT Implementation Manual* (Productivity Press, 1990)—This two-volume manual is a comprehensive, illustrated guide to every aspect of the JIT transformation.

Shigeo Shingo, *A Study of the Toyota Production System from an Industrial Engineering Viewpoint* (Productivity Press, 1989)—This classic book was written by the renowned industrial engineer who helped develop key aspects of its success.

Iwao Kobayashi, *20 Keys to Workplace Improvement* (Productivity Press, 1995)—This book addresses 20 key areas in which a company must improve to maintain a world class manufacturing operation. A five-step improvement for each key is described and illustrated.

The 5S System and Visual Management

The 5S System (Tel-A-Train, 1997)—Filmed at leading U.S. companies, this seven-tape training package (coproduced with Productivity Press) teaches shopfloor teams how to implement the 5S system.

Productivity Press Development Team, *5S for Operators* (Productivity Press, 1996)—This Shopfloor Series book outlines five key principles for creating a clean, visually organized workplace that is easy and safe to work in. Contains numerous tools, illustrated examples, and how-to steps, as well as discussion questions and other learning features.

Michel Greif, *The Visual Factory: Building Participation Through Shared Information* (Productivity Press, 1991)—This book shows how visual management techniques can provide "just-in-time" information to support teamwork and employee participation on the factory floor.

Poka-Yoke (Mistake-Proofing) and Zero Quality Control

Productivity Press Development Team, *Mistake-Proofing for Operators* (Productivity Press, 1997)—This Shopfloor Series book describes the basic theory behind mistake-proofing and introduces poka-yoke systems for preventing errors that lead to defects.

Shigeo Shingo, *Zero Quality Control: Source Inspection and the Poka-Yoke System* (Productivity Press, 1986)—This classic book tells how Shingo developed his ZQC approach and describes the thinking behind its elements. It includes a detailed introduction to poka-yoke devices and many examples of their application in different situations.

NKS/Factory Magazine, ed., *Poka-Yoke: Improving Product Quality by Preventing Defects* (Productivity Press, 1988)—This illustrated book shares 240 poka-yoke examples implemented at different companies to prevent errors and defects.

Quick Changeover

Productivity Press Development Team, *Quick Changeover for Operators* (Productivity Press, 1996)—This Shopfloor Series book describes the stages of changeover improvement with examples and illustrations.

Shigeo Shingo, *A Revolution in Manufacturing: The SMED System* (Productivity Press, 1985)—This classic book tells the story of Shingo's SMED system, tells how to implement it, and provides many changeover improvement examples.

Total Productive Maintenance

Japan Institute of Plant Maintenance, ed., *TPM for Every Operator* (Productivity Press, 1996)—This Shopfloor Series book introduces basic concepts of TPM, with emphasis on the six big equipment-related losses, autonomous maintenance activities, and safety.

Japan Institute of Plant Maintenance, ed., *Autonomous Maintenance for Operators* (Productivity Press, 1997)—This Shopfloor Series book on key autonomous maintenance activities includes chapters on cleaning/inspection, lubrication, localized containment of contamination, and one-point lessons related to maintenance.

Newsletters

For more information about the following publications, call 1-800-966-5423.

Productivity Newsletter—News and case studies on how companies are adopting the lean philosophy and techniques.

Total Employee Involvement (TEI) Newsletter—Describes how smart organizations engage all employees in management and continuous improvement of their processes.

Total Productive Maintenance (TPM) Newsletter—Innovative and up-to-date information on TPM implementation in North America and abroad.

Training and Consulting

Productivity Consulting Group offers a full range of consulting and training services on just-in-time and other manufacturing improvement approaches. For additional information, call 1-800-966-5423.

About the Productivity Press Development Team

Since 1981, Productivity Press has been finding and publishing the world's best methods for achieving manufacturing excellence. At the core of this effort is a team of dedicated editors and writers who work tirelessly to deliver to our customers the most valuable information available on continuous improvement. Their various backgrounds—English literature, graphic design, instructional design, law, library science, psychology, philosophy, and publishing—provide a breadth of knowledge and interests that informs all their work. They love beautiful books and work to create pleasing designs that make the content easy to grasp. They learn continuously about new terminology and changes in both the manufacturing and the publishing industry. They also learn from customers and use this knowledge to create effective books and off-the-shelf products for the learning needs of every level in the organization.

LEARNING PACKAGE

The Learning Package is designed to give your team leaders everything they need to facilitate study groups on *Just-in-Time for Operators*. Shopfloor workers participate through a series of discussion and application sessions to practice using the tools and techniques they've learned from the book.

The Learning Package:

- Provides the foundation for launching a full-scale implementation process
- Provides immediate practical skills for participants
- Offers a flexible course design you can adapt to your unique requirements
- Encourages workers to become actively involved in their own learning process

Included In Your Learning Package:

- Five copies of *Just-in-Time for Operators*
- One copy of *Kanban: Just-in-Time at Toyota*
- One 8-1/2" x 11" Leader's Guide
- A set of overhead transparencies that summarize major points
- A set of slides with case study examples

Just-in-time for Operators Learning Package
The Productivity Press Development Team
ISBN 1-56327-134-6
Item # JITLP-B8001

About the Shopfloor Series

Put powerful and proven improvement tools in the hands of your entire workforce!

Progressive shopfloor improvement techniques are imperative for manufacturers who want to stay competitive and to achieve world class excellence. And it's the comprehensive education of all shopfloor workers that ensures full participation and success when implementing new programs. The Shopfloor Series books make practical information accessible to everyone by presenting major concepts and tools in simple, clear language and at a reading level that has been adjusted for operators by skilled instructional designers. One main idea is presented every two to four pages so that the book can be picked up and put down easily. Each chapter begins with an overview and ends with a summary section. Helpful illustrations are used throughout.

Books currently in the Shopfloor Series include:

5S FOR OPERATORS
5 Pillars of the Visual Workplace
The Productivity Press Development Team
ISBN 1-56327-123-0 /
incl. application questions / 133 pages
Order 5SOP-B8001 / $25.00

QUICK CHANGEOVER FOR OPERATORS
The SMED System
The Productivity Press Development Team
ISBN 1-56327-125-7 /
incl. application questions / 93 pages
Order QCOOP-B8001 / $25.00

MISTAKE-PROOFING FOR OPERATORS
The Productivity Press Development Team
ISBN 1-56327-127-3 / 93 pages
Order ZQCOP-B8001 / $25.00

TPM FOR SUPERVISORS
The Productivity Press Development Team
ISBN 1-56327-161-3 / 96 pages
Order TPMSUP-B8001 / $25.00

TPM TEAM GUIDE
Kunio Shirose
ISBN 1-56327-079-X / 175 pages
Order TGUIDE-B8001 / $25.00

TPM FOR EVERY OPERATOR
The Japan Institute of Plant Maintenance
ISBN 1-56327-080-3 / 136 pages
Order TPMEO-B8001 / $25.00

AUTONOMOUS MAINTENANCE
The Japan Institute of Plant Maintenance
ISBN 1-56327-082-x / 138 pages
Order AUTOMOP-B8001 / $25.00

FOCUSED EQUIPMENT IMPROVEMENT FOR TPM TEAMS
The Japan Institute of Plant Maintenance
ISBN 1-56327-081-1 / 144 pages
Order FEIOP-B8001 / $25.00

Productivity Press, Dept. BK, P.O. Box 13390. Portland, OR 97213-0390
Telephone: **1-800-394-6868** Fax **1-800-394-6286**

CONTINUE YOUR LEARNING WITH IN-HOUSE TRAINING AND CONSULTING FROM THE PRODUCTIVITY CONSULTING GROUP

The Productivity Consulting Group (PCG) offers a diverse menu of consulting services and training products based on the exciting ideas contained in the books of Productivity Press. Whether you need assistance with long term planning or focused, results-driven training, PCG's experienced professional staff can enhance your pursuit of competitive advantage.

PCG integrates a cutting edge management system with today's leading process improvement tools for rapid, measurable, lasting results. In concert with your management team, PCG will focus on implementing the principles of Value Adding Management, Total Quality Management, Just-In-Time, and Total Productive Maintenance. Each approach is supported by Productivity's wide array of team-based tools: Standardization, One-Piece Flow, Hoshin Planning, Quick Changeover, Mistake-Proofing, Kanban, Problem Solving with CEDAC, Visual Workplace, Visual Office, Autonomous Maintenance, Equipment Effectiveness, Design of Experiments, Quality Function Deployment, Ergonomics, and more. And, based on the continuing research of Productivity Press, PCG expands its offerings every year.

Productivity is known for significant improvement on the shopfloor and the bottom line. Through years of repeat business, an expanding and loyal client base continues to recommend Productivity to their colleagues. Contact PCG to learn how we can tailor our services to fit your needs.

Telephone: 1-800-966-5423 (U. S. only) or 1-203-846-3777
Fax: 1-203-846-6883

READING

THE FOUNDATIONAL SKILL OF THE KNOWLEDGE WORKER

In keeping with our vision as "The Education Company for the Knowledge Era", Productivity Press has developed an affiliation with READ RIGHT, a company specializing in workforce literacy. If members of the workforce in your company have difficulty reading this book, we recommend you consult READ RIGHT for assistance.

 ### Read Right Specializing in Workforce Literacy
Eliminating employee reading problems yields hidden benefits

A breakthrough that helps employees quickly eliminate reading problems and improve English communication skills is yielding very encouraging side benefits. Not only are graduates of READ RIGHT able to read and understand training materials, safety signs, equipment manuals, and other written communications—they also realize new feelings of self-confidence and self-esteem. This translates into greater willingness to become involved in team meetings. With new skills and self-confidence, workers participate, speak up, and contribute ideas as never before.

"We see people who were once reluctant to participate on teams for Total Quality Improvement projects now stepping up. I see people coming out of their shells and coming forward with more improvement ideas. I can think of no other training we have done or are doing that will make a greater contribution to improving the performance of our mills than READ RIGHT."

— Otto Lueschel, Vice President, Manufacturing, Weyerhaeuser, Western Lumber Division

New knowledge about how the brain learns the reading process has enabled READ RIGHT to develop a fundamentally new way to teach reading that cuts the time necessary to eliminate employees' reading problems by over 90%. READ RIGHT is also effective in teaching English communication skills to employees for whom English is a second language.

For more information on how READ RIGHT might benefit your employees and your company, please phone 1-800-427-9440.